Jiggery-Pokery

Semicentennial

Jiggery-Pokery

Semicentennial

EDITED BY

Daniel Groves & Greg Williamson

WITH A RE-INTRODUCTION BY

Willard Spiegelman

WAYWISER

First published in 2017 by

THE WAYWISER PRESS

Christmas Cottage, Church Enstone, Chipping Norton, Oxfordshire, OX7 4NN, UK
P.O. Box 6205, Baltimore, MD 21206, USA
https://waywiser-press.com

Editor-in-Chief
Philip Hoy

Senior American Editor
Joseph Harrison

Associate Editors
Eric McHenry | Dora Malech | V. Penelope Pelizzon | Clive Watkins
Greg Williamson | Matthew Yorke

This compendium © Daniel Groves and Greg Williamson 2017
The Introduction © Willard Spiegelman, 2017
Copyright of the poems featured in this anthology rests with the authors

The right of Daniel Groves and Greg Williamson to be identified as the editors
of this work has been asserted by them in accordance with the
Copyright, Designs and Patents Act of 1988.

All rights reserved. No part of this publication may be reproduced, stored in a
retrieval system, or transmitted in any form or by any means, electronic,
mechanical, photocopying, recording, or otherwise, without the prior permission
of both the copyright owner and the above publisher of this book.

9 7 5 3 1 2 4 6 8

A CIP catalogue record for this book is available from the British Library

ISBN 978-1-904130-88-8

Printed and bound by
T. J. International Ltd., Padstow, Cornwall, PL28 8RW

i.m. Anthony Hecht and John Hollander

JIGGERY-POKERY: A RE-INTRODUCTION

Here's something poets and readers of poetry should consider: the relationship between poetic voice and poetic form. How often does a new poetic type swim into our ken, arrive on the scene unannounced? When, and why? If poets are concerned, not to say obsessed, with "finding their voices" and staking claims to originality, why do so few of them make new forms, forms that other poets can take up, imitate, play with, and make their own? Voice and form are allies.

The origins of poetic genres are mostly shrouded in the mists of history. Who invented the sonnet, the sestina, the villanelle, or even blank verse? Who in Japan invented the haiku? The polls have not closed on the question. Less enduring forms have known makers but are seldom imitated. Robert Pack has given us *Rounding It Out*, his volume of "sonnettelles" (1999), a portmanteau meshing of the sonnet and the villanelle. More recently, we have Tyehimba Jess's "syncopated sonnets" and other divided lyrics combining hip hop performance and poems written for two voices that can be articulated variously: one voice on the left, one on the right, or the two mingled straight through. A similar but denser and more baroque form comes from Greg Williamson: the "double exposure" (2000), which is really three separate poems without reference to clear human identities: lines in standard type make up one poem; they alternate with lines in boldface, which make a second poem. The third combines the two separate ones, now read from start to finish, a *durchkomponiert* whole that is greater than the sum of its two parts. Whew.

But most of the new forms of the past several centuries belong to the family we vaguely label "light verse." Why is this so? They sit squarely, according to the division proposed by the late John Hollander in his elegant and magisterial *Rhyme's Reason*, in the column of "verse," not "authentic "poetry" proper. That is, they call our attention to matters of music and structure rather than to metaphor and trope. And they are fun. The limerick appeared in the early eighteenth century, but it didn't take hold and flourish until the following one. In the waning days of Victorian and Edwardian nonsense, Edmund Clerihew Bentley gave us his own eponymous light verse quatrains.

And then: the kind of poems presented in the sly volume of glittering folderol you see before you. Fifty years ago Hollander and Anthony Hecht, both playful masters of poetic form, cornered the market on the double dactyl in *Jiggery-Pokery* (1967). Hecht, with Paul Pascal, had actually invented the form in 1951. He tells the amusing story of the accidental genesis of the poem in his part of the introduction to the book. Countless evenings of parlor poets intoning "Higgledy-Piggledy" ensued. Think of "Mad Libs" but with higher stakes. To readers new to the form in the twenty-first century, I repeat the original requirements: the poem has two quatrains, with lines four and eight rhyming; the first three lines of each stanza consist of two dactylic feet; the fourth is a truncated, four-syllable line; the first line is a nonsense combination of words, perhaps relevant to the subject that follows. And finally: one line must be a proper name, and one must be a single, twelve-syllable, double dactyl.

Got that?

In the twenty-first century, many strict forms, including the resonant villanelle and sestina, can frequently look like deliberate exercises in clever archaism, or scintillating extensions of frivolity. (There are notable exceptions. One cannot find anything archaic in Theodore Roethke's "The Waking," Dylan Thomas's "Do Not Go Gentle Into That Good Night," or Elizabeth Bishop's "One Art," all canonical.) Often they belong more to the workshop than to the free choices of mature poets. Can they be serious, or are they fated to be mere pyrotechnics? After the ascendancy of free verse, as Dana Gioia pointed out years ago, the simple fact of rhyme, and any meter other than the historically sanctioned iambic pentameter were delegated to the lower realms of *vers de société*, to *The New Yorker*, to greeting cards, to the tribe of Longfellow and more minor historical figures who have passed from popularity. Blank verse maintained a seriousness of effect, thanks to Shakespeare, Milton, and Wordsworth; more jaunty meters seemed less weighty, less vital. They could not be harnessed to the reins of sobriety or purposefulness.

Let's consider the question from another angle. Think of "light verse" not as mere triviality but as a special form of illumination. The double dactyl makes its own claims, and does its own work. It has grown over time. Take a look at the following pages: you will find God's plenty, wittily miniaturized. The new double dactyls collected by Messrs. Groves and Williamson prove individually and collectively that having once "learned" the rules of the form, a poet may produce a learnèd work, a poem both "simple, sensuous, and passionate" (Milton's desideratum) and playful, witty, even intellectual. Milton is not exactly the first person one thinks of when contemplating "simplicity" in poetry. But like all great poets, he can put wit and intellect at the service of the senses.

The poets in these pages have extended the boundaries of Hecht and Hollander's original definitions, and of their anthology of half a century ago. One hopes that the old masters would have approved, rather than disdained, newer variations on the form. These have been committed in the spirit, if not the letter, of the original. Surely the originators made their initial prescriptions with tongue at least partly in cheek: "[P]resently, and probably very soon, the very supply of double dactylic words in all languages will have been exhausted, bringing the form to its ultimate demise." The idea being, of course, that the single double dactylic word, appearing preferably in the antepenultimate line of the eight-line poem, could never appear again in any other poet's contribution. This claim threw down the gauntlet to following generations. Over the past fifty years, poets, poetasters, and genial amateurs alike have picked it up. They have picked up, as well, the Hecht-Hollander hope that the use of appropriate foreign words might help to revive macaronic verse, a form mostly unused since the Middle Ages.

The originators sometimes called themselves "Anthony Hollander." They also styled themselves the "Regents," the rule makers. They were uncertain about the use of hyphenation in the creation of single-lined double dactyls, which the reader of this book will find used liberally by today's practitioners. What the founders would not have foreseen was the ubiquity, in twenty-first century America, of hyphenations of identity—African-American, Asian-American, Hispanic-American, and even triple rather than double hyphenated sorts—that would also encourage the creative use of linguistic gamesmanship to reflect a polyglot world in print as well as speech. Whether this new convention represents a natural development from, or a depletion of, the original form, will remain moot until the next generation of double-dactylists comes along.

Contained in this slim volume, readers will find poems that are didactic, secular, witty, and ironic, as well as illuminating: often sensuous and passionate, perhaps even simple. Their illumination comes, in fact, from their didactic wit. Among the extenders or violators of the form is James Cummins ("Old Possum"), who manages a triple rhyme in his first stanza while simultaneously adding a (normally or previously forbidden?) extra syllable to lines 4 and 8. A. M. Juster ("Cowed") also uses rhymes in lines other than 4 and 8, but he maintains the traditional four-syllables of each stanza's ultimate line. Throughout these pages the patient ordinary reader may find work that sends him or her to the dictionary (English or otherwise) or the encyclopedia: let "Freundschaftsbezeigungen," "Neo-monophysite," "cacoepy," "Joshua Chamberlain," "Frederick Mellinger," and "John Streeter Manifold" stand in for others.

In addition, the Regents' fear that hyphens might be used too liberally has borne fruit—whether tasty, or dangerously and genetically modified remains to be determined by each reader's *gustibus*: "Garden-variety"; "Gastro-omnisciently" (this thing of darkness I acknowledge mine); "Quantum-mechanically"; "Saccharo-oligarch"; "Medi-neologist"; the possibly controversial "Scopophile-aide-de-leer," which has the delicious double distinction of being confected as well as punningly polyglot; and many others.

And yet as the form perhaps deforms itself it also enriches itself. Consider, finally, Sean Kelly's supremely confident contribution, a far-from-embarrassing extension that goes beyond the form's boundaries without violating them:

> Hocusy-pocusy
> Padre Bogoglio
> Ecclestiastical
> Papal dark horse,
>
> Pontifex Maximus,
> Anachronistically
> Semipelagian—
> Hopeless, of course.

"Hopeless?" Certainly not. The radical theology and media-friendly social tactics of Pope Francis have met their match as well as an appropriate conveyance in the playful expansions of poetic systems. The rules of the double dactyl game are not inscribed in stone. Canons change. In Kelly's eight-line gem we have two proper names, and three single-lined double dactyls: it's a maximalist double-dactyl, if ever there was one. Even the prescribed nonsensical opening line mouths any modern skeptic's doubts concerning the Holy Roman Church and its seemingly arcane rituals. Sean Kelly has found his voice through an experiment with a form. One can only wonder what will come next.

Willard Spiegelman

MALE GAZE

Jiggery-Pokery
Orpheus Porphyry
What were you thinking then,
Turning your head?

Love is perdition that
Eurydicedingly
Lingers in hindsight: she's
Better off dead.

Kevin Craft

THE SONG OF ROLAND

Gallopy-Wallopy
Roland and Oliver
Riding at Roncevals
Died for a *Song*.

Ollie died rapidly;
Rollie, more slowly, for
Auto-encomiums
Ought to last long.

John DuVal

HADRIAN'S HOPE

Jiggery-Pokery
Emperor Hadrian
Ordered the Pantheon
Built for his fame.

But for MacDonald's book,
Architectonically,
Who in the world
Would remember his name?

Judith Testa

ENGLAND, MY (BUT MOSTLY YOUR) ENGLAND

>Sherwoody Foresty
>Robin-and-Marian's
>Redistributional
>Plans for the rich
>
>Promised the poor their fair
>Share of the commonwealth—
>Minus some service fees…
>Son of a bitch.

Brad Leithauser

VENETIAN FANCIES

Pains-taking, Paint-making,
Victor Carpaccio
Lived in the Renaissance
Near the Lagoon.

"Plates of thin beef," he said
 Gastro-omnisciently,
"Feeding the rich, will be
 Named for me soon."

Willard Spiegelman

COWED

Romanov Stroganov
Ivan the Terrible
Grew so unbearable
Peasants were riled.

Counterinsurgencies
Compromised urgencies
Calling for scarable
"Ivan the Mild."

A. M. Juster

HARINGTON, JOHN

Gloucestershire Worcestershire
Knighted John Harington
Wrote noble epigrams,
Yet is renowned

For an invention more
Worldtransformational:
Namely, the privy
Where excrement's drowned.

X. J. Kennedy

AT CULLODEN

Porky yet masterful,
Sweet Butcher Cumberland,
Third son of German George
(Second of name),

Killed many highlanders,
Extrajudicially.
Sheep eat the weeds named for
Him all the same.

Guy Benjamin Brookshire

IN MEMORIAM CERVARUM

Mambiness Bambiness
Alfred Lord Tennyson[1]
Hankered for venison
Braised in weak beer.

Brisket would thicken him;
Chicken would sicken him.
Seafood of any fin
Lost out to deer.

A. M. Juster

LITERARY CORRESPONDENCE (DISTILLED)

> T. Wentworth Higginson,[2a]
> Emily Dickinson's
> Philistine pen-pal, dis-
> Counted her song.
>
> Out on circumference
> She feigned indifference,
> Incontrovertibly
> Proving him wrong.

Jacqueline Osherow

THE DISASTER

Doggerel Doggerel
William McGonagall
Worst poet ever
To pick up a pen—

Trying to wade through his
Ultra-incompetent
Verses will make you say, "Fuck it, I'll never get sucked
    into reading a poem
Again."

Austin Allen

CHAMBERLAIN

Hickory Dickory
Joshua Chamberlain,
Scholar of rhetoric,
Called, "Bayonet!"

Routing the Rebels, he
Anti-rhetorically
Proved that concision is
One's better bet.

Philip Stephens

1789

Dash-away Dash-away
Emily Dickinson[2b]
Stayed—home—in Amherst and
Flew in her—Words,

Crafting a—Universe
Irreconcilable
Except we learn how—She
Sings—Us—like Birds.

Annie Finch

HUMPERDINCK

Pat-a-cake Pat-a-cake
Engelbert Humperdinck
Didn't sing pop songs or
Pump Heavy Metal.

Though such a fact may seem
Contra-indicative,
He wrote an opera:
Hänsel und Gretel.

John Fuller

VON HOFMANNSTHAL

Higgledy-Piggledy
Hugo von Hofmannsthal[3]
Wrote hushed libretti for
Noisy Herr Strauss,

Radiant fables that
Incomprehensibly
Lifted the spirit and
Brought down the house.

J. D. McClatchy

LADY DADA

"Coitus is paramount"
Baroness Elsa von
Freytag, etc.
Wunderbar scamp

Set an example of
Freundschaftsbezeigungen
Mailing a toilet to
Marcel Duchamp.

Jaimee Hills

MOORE

Boom-shaka Boom-shaka
Disliking poetry
Tri-cornered-hat-wearing
Marianne Moore

Called for an end but said,
"Improbabilistically,
Lizards in liquorice—
That I adore."

William Logan

OLD POSSUM

Jelly it Jelly it
Thomas Stearns Eliot,[4]
Sometimes indelicate,
Peu epicene-y:

Walrus or Lear, *poly-*
Phyloprogenitive's
Spirit of Lennon, not
Paraclete Sweeney.

James Cummins

TOLKIEN

Higgledy-Piggledy
J. R. R. Tolkien
Lost in a landscape
Of trees, hills, and dales.

So much time given to
Rings-that-are-Precious:
Better to stop this
And just go to Zales.

Kim Bridgford

DEEP IN DEEP ELLUM

Tappety Tappety
Blind Lemon Jefferson,
Jived drunks and hustlers with
"'Lectric Chair Blues."

Thanatological
Fretting concluded, he
Called for his wages in
Coochie and booze.

Andrew Hudgins

THE FULTON SHEEN PROGRAM

Hymn-a-nee Bim-a-nee
Archbishop Fulton Sheen,
Prince of All Media,
But not his church,

Trends now to sainthood, a
Televangelical
Kinescoped relic his
Death can't besmirch.

Andrew Hudgins

IF I LOVED YOU

Dah-da-da Dah-da-da
Rodgers and Hammerstein
Working together were
Doomed from the start.

Musical liberal
Sentimentality
Never could beat out a
Song with a Hart.

J. Kates

A LESSON FROM THE MASTER

Хокеры Хокеры
Vladimir Nabokov[5]
Can't abide people who
Garble his name:

"Try to pronounce it *Vla-
DE-mir Na-BO-kof*. A-
Merican accents are
Really quite lame."

Charles Martin

CERTAINLY NOT

Hysteron Proteron
Werner Karl Heisenberg
Felt that his birthday was
Hard to endure:

Could he eat cake now and,
Quantum-mechanically,
Save it for afterwards?
He wasn't sure.

David Yezzi

FAREWELL TO THE ONE LUMP OR TWO

Cubity Cubity
Benjamin Eisenstadt,
Sweet-N-Low wizard who
Pitched us the woo.

Cursed sachet-maker,
Saccharo-oligarch
Packaging seven grams,
Substance just two.

Michael Griffith

DEATH INVADES THE DUCHY

Pilgrima Pilgrima
Marion Morrison
Known to the world by the
John and the *Wayne*,

Gets not his due as a
Medi-neologist,
But "the Big C" brought him
Glory, and pain.

Michael Griffith

MUSICAL MYSTERY TOUR

Higgledy-Piggledy
Herbert von Karajan,
Asked by his cab driver:
"Where to, mein Herr?"

"Take me to Paris … or
Czechoslovakia …
You make the choice, I'm a
Star everywhere."

Willard Spiegelman

SONNY BOY WILLIAMSON II

Ol' Mr. So-and-So,
Sonny Boy Williamson
Borrowed a moniker
Meant to confuse,

Using its crowd appeal
Self-referentially,
Gaining an audience,
Playing the blues.

Alfred Nicol

DIMAGGIO

Son of a fisherman,
Vincent DiMaggio,
Drawn by the lure of the
Diamond mystique,

Quit the sea, jolting the
Paterfamilias;
Kid brother Joe shared his
Obstinate streak.

Alfred Nicol

OVERLORD OF THE UNDERWIRE

Hummina Hummina
Frederick Mellinger
Lingerie magnate, up-
Pusher of bras,

Gravity's enemy,
Scopophile-aide-de-leer,
Ta-ta to privacy,
Hi to ta-tas.

Michael Griffith

A PEARL-HANDLED MODEL FIVE WALTHER 6.35

Not-a-see, Odd-a-see
Unity Walkyrie
Mitford was thrilled by the
Gift Hitler brought:

Out of its barrel at
Hypervelocity
Shot through her dura her
First and last thought.

Andrew Hudgins

MANIFOLD

Higgledy-Piggledy
John Streeter Manifold
Knew from his cradle the
Shape of a horse;

Having found World War II
Ideological,
Turned back to verse and penned
Ballads, of course.

Christopher Wallace-Crabbe

FOR THE SCHOLAR WHO WROTE
SURREALISM: THE ROAD TO THE ABSOLUTE,
AND
ANDRÉ BRETON: MAGUS OF SURREALISM

    Pocketa Pocketa
    Anna Balakian
    Rode to the absolute
    Pure psychic zone,

    Non-automatically
    Writing her bio of
    Big-shot surrealist
    André Breton.

John Drury

BE CATCHIN' UP ON THE REBOUND WITH THE MEDICIDE

"Subba say I wan' see"
Barbara Billingsley,
Ward's being "hard on the
Beaver last night,"

Later was cast as a
Sexagenarian
Speaker of jive on one
Ill-fêted flight.

Greg Williamson

THE DUCHESS'S WAY

Gibbledy Gabbledy
Deborah Cavendish,
Last of the Mitford girls,
aged ninety-four,

Aristocratically
Cut the Grim Reaper dead:
"Go back to Venice you
Crushing old bore."

David Yezzi

FOR CAROL, THE HEROINE OF *MAIN STREET*

> Bippity Boppity
> Mrs. Will Kennicott
> Found Gopher Prairie a
> Philistine hell.
>
> Incontrovertible
> Proof now exists, though, that
> Sinclair the Laureate
> Thought it was swell.

John Drury

KISSINGER

Higgledy-Piggledy
Henry A. Kissinger
Picked up the Peace Prize
Bestowed by Nobel;

Dante[6] observed that such
Hyper-hypocrisy
Transmits the sinner
Directly to Hell.

Sean Kelly

WITH A WAVE OF THE WAND

Bibbity Bobbity
Walt Disney Studios
Gave the world fairy-tale
Magic and awe

Packaged in Happy Meals,
Animatronically
Programmed, and claimed
Under copyright law.

Austin Allen

ETERNAL VIGILANCE

Searching for heretics,
Jaroslav Pelikan,
Keeper of Orthodox
Values, would pray,

"Lord let me challenge and
Utterly vanquish a
Neo-monophysite,
Sometime today."

Charles Martin

DR. LOVE

Hugging his audience,
Leo Buscaglia
Peddled his pablum on
Public TV;

Frustrated makers of
Antibacterial
Soap couldn't advertise,
Fortunately.

Alfred Nicol

$$Z_{N+1} = Z_N^2 + C$$

Fractally Dactylly
Sir Benoit Mandelbrot
Folded the universe
Into a rose,

Fragrantly, *flagrantly*,
Autopoietically
Ordering entropy
Under our nose.

Jennifer Maier

POINT MADE

Oochity Ouchity
Yukio Mishima
Worked as a model when
Not writing prose.

Clearly Sebasuchan
Eschatologically
Pierced through the abdomen
Wasn't a pose.

David Yezzi

KEVORKIAN

Hickory Dickory
Doctor Kevorkian,
Lately of Michigan,
Built a machine.

Lacking a patent, he
Unsuicidally
Prospered from patients he
Rendered serene.

John Drury

TARGET DEMOGRAPHIC

Penis and labia,
Dr. Ruth Westheimer,
Sniper of note in the
Second World War,

Aimed her remarks at an
Ultraconservative
Radio audience.
Many got sore.

Greg Williamson

JACKIE DOES DALLAS

Hey hey ha, Nah nah nee,
Jacqueline Bouvier[7]
Wouldn't have married no
Regular Joe.

Destined to greet the world
Aristocratically,
Strawberry pink Chanel
Suit fit for … O.

Hastings Hensel

LGBT

Cosily-craftily
Victor/Victoria
Thought s/he would try on some
New negligées.

Preening, admiring
Hermaphroditically,
V/V said "watch me go
Out in a blaze."

Willard Spiegelman

RAMBLIN' JACK

Flibbity Jibbity
Ramblin' Jack Elliott
Flipped out on Brooklyn and
Rodeo shows,

When he showed up again,
Hypertheatrically,
He was part Guthrie, part
Lasso, part clothes.

Terese Coe

SAME CAT TIME, OR DYNAMIC DO-OVER, OR WEST/WARD *HAUTE*

Kittenish kitschiness,
Julia Newmeyer
Chatted- (and hipped-) up the
Goth, *pour l'amour,*

Tailored to turn heads, and
(Novemmortality?)
Dressed to the nines, as if
Newly Lamarr.

Daniel Groves

"…THE ONE"

WHOA-oh-whoa, YEAH-oh-yeah,
Sylvia Robinson—
Broken glass everywhere
(Post-vocal range)—

Flashed-back delighted as
Sylvia Vanderpool
*Rap*port-producingly
Mused "Love is Strange."

Daniel Groves

SCALIA

"Jiggery-pokery!
 Pure applesaucery!"
Antonin Gregory
Jeered from the bench,

Using the same words I
Involuntarily
Yelped when the eulogist
Called him a mensch.

Eric McHenry

YES

Trumpery, trumpery!
Senator John McCain
Hearing *heroic* means
Not getting caught

Caught himself wondering
Unpresidentially
Can this twit be even
Worse than I thought?

Gilbert Allen

POPE FRANCIS

Hocusy Pocusy
Padre Bergoglio
Ecclesiastical
Papal dark horse,

Pontifex Maximus,
Anachronistically
Semipelagian—
Hopeless, of course.

Sean Kelly

STARK WEATHER

Higgledy-Piggledy
Charlie R. Starkweather,
Teased for cacoepy,
Shocked the Midwest.

Road-enraged rhotacist
(Wuh-wuh-wuh-whoa-tacist!),
Mocked with impunity
Since his awwest.

Andrew Hudgins

THE GODFATHER

Bippity Boppety
Francis Ford Coppola
Bucked crazy Paramount
Shooting Part I:

Held out for Marlon, who
Characteristically
Clobbered the moguls and
Answered to none.

Terese Coe

LATE DYLAN

Hibbinga Cribbinga
Robert A. Zimmerman's
Eschatological
Visions begat

Merely a menacing
Irascability
Which sounded only the
Better for that.

Robert Schreur

THE HAIRY MAN WHO APPEARS AS A SYMPTOM OF DESTRUCTION (BLUFF CREEK, CA 1967)

Hairy Man Woodbooger
Robert Heironimus
Claims it was *he* Roger
Captured on tape,

Hoax or not, jumpstarting
Cryptozoology's
Search for the secretive
Stinkaboo Ape.

Greg Williamson

BLINKY

"Grouseleachy," "housebeachy,"
 Frederick Biletnikoff
 Heard in the huddle from
 Snake with his drawl,

One-handed snag, *a, a*
 Parthenogenesis,[8]
 Mullet on fire, his
 Mustache a maul.

Adam Vines

ROBINSON

Higgledy-Piggledy
Marilynne Robinson
Shouldn't have found her name
Here, where I hid it,

But she was googling
"Teleological
Monograph dealers near
Me," and that did it.

Eric McHenry

HEY, THAT BEER COST TWELVE BUCKS!

Splishity Damn-it-all
Krazy George Henderson,
Shock-headed cheerer,
Invented "the Wave,"

Spoiler of lager, pep's
Foam-finger-fascism,
Why must the lap-laden
Rise as a slave?

Michael Griffith

TRUMP

Higgledy-Piggledy
Donald Phallacious
Brings back elections to
Homecoming court.

No time for subtlety
(Hit-on-the-headery):
Just calls to greatness
And not to abort.

Kim Bridgford

MAKE THE PIE HIGHER FATHERS

Jiggery-Pokery
43rd President
AKA Dubya, played
Thief of Baghdad.

That proved a bit of a
Misunderestimate
(So thought his Father, and
Also his Dad.)

Richard Kenney

IT'S MORE THAN JUST A DRESS

Brick-a-tee Brack-a-let
Diane von Furstenberg
Gave us a cotton sack
Cinched at the waist,

Clambered from princess to
Uber-couturier,
Deep-sixed her umlaut, a
Matter of taste.

Natalie Shapero

HEAD OVER HEELS OVER, OR CALL IT IN THE AIR

Richard "Dick" Fosbury,
Sidestepping rectitude
(Raising the bar, *per se*—
Over-the-top

Foresight), leapt backward to
Proto-ascendency;
Converts half-flipped as we
Coined it a "flop."

Daniel Groves

MS. CALCULATEDLY

"Arkansas, schmarkansas,"
 Candidate Hillary
 Smirked when a journalist
 Asked if she'd win it.

"Six electoral votes?
 Razorbassackwardness?
 Gave up all that in a
 Hot New York minute."

Geoffrey Brock

ON THE QUI VIVE

Tickety Tockety
Vladimir, Estragon,
Waited too long for a
Mr. Godot.

When they got hungry they
Archmasochistically
Ate their philosophy
Sans the Bordeaux.

Terese Coe

SOUND CHECK

Higgledy-Piggledy
Michael D. Huckabee
Running for president
Wants to be liked.

So he won't answer to
Ultraformality.
When he is speaking he
Asks to be "Miked."

J. Kates

GENDER TROUBLE

Kris, the Kardashians'
Man-handler/ Momager's
Heteronormative
Botox regime

Coupled with Jenner-bent
Bruce's transition makes
Phallogocentrism
Seem less extreme.

Brian Brodeur

MY FIFTEEN MINUTES

Pishero Poshero
Jacqueline Osherow
Shamelessly scribbles
Her dactylic name,

Uncomplicatedly
(If too belatedly)
Hoping to jumpstart her
Poetic fame.

Jacqueline Osherow

POST-SACK, OR NIELSEN RATING, OR "THE BUSINESS DOWN THERE..."

>Big market bell-ringer
>Marcus Dell Gastineau,
>Having to each of them
>Given his seat,
>
>Shares an exchange as yet
>Non-penalizable—
>First with the quarterback,
>Then with Brigitte.

Daniel Groves

ALL I'M ASKING FOR IS WHAT I WANT

    Hey batter, swing batter,
    Rickey H. Henderson,
    All-time base stealer, sent
    Rickey this memo:

"Rickey don't," Rickey said,
  Illeisterical,
"Like it when Rickey can't
  Find Rickey's limo."

Greg Williamson

GIRLS CAN DO ANYTHING!

Golly gee willickers
Barbara Millicent
(Not too receptive to
"Barbie" these days)

Thinks, as a stewardess-
Veterinarian-
Lifeguard-and-rapper she's
Earned a damn raise.

Caki Wilkinson

PEACE IS CLOSER

Nnnn…Oom…eh, Oh yeah yeah,
W. Axl Rose,
Bandannaed Aphid, gave
Gn'FR

Chinese Democracy
(Pop-paradoxical),
Using allusions to
Civil F War.

Hastings Hensel

DIVADIENST

Do-re-mi Do-re-mi
Angela Gheorghiu,
"Yes," to Puccini said;
"No way" to Bach;

"Masses and Passions are too
Kapellmeisterisch.
Lutheran doom and gloom
Don't fit my fach."

Kenneth Bleeth

PIRATED

Buoyant resurfacings:
Pamela Anderson,
Peered—in one (tight) piece, still—
Out on the blue

(Deep focus) scene of a
Horizontality
Tacking to leeward with
What motley crew.

Daniel Groves

WEEKLY WORLD NEWS
(DATELINE HOLLYWOOD)

Jiggery-Pokery
Jennifer Aniston
Sheds off her snakeskin for
Vanity Fair;

Lizard-brain pleasures are
Garden-variety;
Knock on our crania:
Nobody's there.

Cody Walker

AND THE ANSWER IS NOT A GAME, NOT A GAME

Crossover Crossover,
Allen E. Iverson,
Never asserting *non*
Est meus actus,

Strove to make clear to the
Semiprofessional
Press conference people, "We're
Talkin' 'bout *practice*!"

Greg Williamson

COMPUTATION

Higgledy-Piggledy
Benedict Cumberbatch
Played Alan Turing, an
Asperger Brit.

Toying with Christopher
Homoerotically
And cryptographically
Challenged his wit.

Willard Spiegelman

E-PISTLE FOR MICHAEL

Bippity Boppity
Michael D. Snediker
Wrote Henry James an e-
Pistle in verse.

"Establishmentarian
Master of Nuance, we
Praise your disdain for the
Pointlessly terse."

Alfred Corn

HANKY FUNKADELIC

Boogaloo Pickety
Sir Nose D'VoidofFunk
Couched on his hinder is
Too cool to dance.

Sofa king sofa king
Anticofunkified
Rhythm runs off with his
Groovyolence.

Jaimee Hills

BLADE RUNNER N' GUNNER

Click-a-clack Clack-a-clink
Oscar Pistorius
Triggered the end to his
Life on the run.

Self-defense claim for a
Dysto-Olympian?
Anxious as always he'd
Sprung at the gun.

Hastings Hensel

GAME OF THRONES

Nollamy Nollamy
Dany Targaryen
Seems to disrobe at the
Drop of a hat.

Queen of the Andals! Our
Leaders by contrast are
Unexhibitionist.
Thank God for that.

James Arthur

WEEKLY WORLD NEWS (DATELINE SEATTLE)

Higgledy-Piggledy
Friday-night Warrior
Funnels a Budweiser,
Crushing the can;

Predestinarian
Doctrine's a bitch but I
See him at Day's End with
Kennewick Man.

Cody Walker

BODY POLITIC

Jiggery-Pokery
Congress bicameral!
Short-term prognosis? Your
Doctors are dour.

What intervention might
Surgery offer you?
Hemicorpectomy:
Honk for the cure.

Richard Kenney

DOUBLE DUCTILE

Wittily whiskery
Anthony Hollander[(TM)9]
Fifty some years ago
burnished a form—

Seriocomically
Polysyllabical—
Which quite unlikelily
Took us by storm.

Brad Leithauser

NOTES

1. cf. "Sources of Juvenile Crime," et al. by Anthony Hecht and John Hollander. *Jiggery-Pokery: A Compendium of Double Dactyls* (Atheneum, 1967), p. 78.

2a & 2b. cf. "Higgledy-Higginson?" by Donald Hall. Ibid., p. 79.

3. cf. "The German Romantics III," by Richard Howard. Ibid., p. 90 (also, cf. "I Go Hugo," by Eugene V. Ellis. *Esquire,* September 1966, p. 88).

4. cf. "Vice," et al., by Anthony Hecht and Christopher Wallace-Crabbe. *Jiggery-Pokery: A Compendium of Double Dactyls* (Atheneum, 1967), p. 93 (also, cf. "Change of Allegiance," by Robley Wilson, Jr. *Esquire*, September 1966, p. 88).

5. cf. "Impressionism," by Christopher Wallace-Crabbe, *Jiggery- Pokery: A Compendium of Double Dactyls* (Atheneum, 1967), p. 95 (also, cf. "Correction," by William Matthews. *Esquire*, September 1966, p. 88).

6. see *Inferno* 33.124-147.

7. cf. "Neo-Classic," by James Merrill. *Jiggery-Pokery: A Compendium of Double Dactyls* (Atheneum, 1967), p. 107.

8. As even a (to a point) deferential purist will detect, while Adam Vines' "Blinky" fulfills the formal requirement, stipulated by Anthony Hecht in his Introduction to the original *Jiggery-Pokery*, of having a "double dactylic line which is *one word long*," it does so by employing a word previously employed by James Merrill's "Above All That?," and thus would

seem to violate a further requirement stipulated by Hecht, that ("and the beauty of the form consists chiefly in this"), "once such a double dactylic word has successfully been employed in this verse form, it may never be used again." We endorse "Blinky" not, assuredly, because we wish to question the success of Merrill's employment of "Parthenogenesis," but indeed because Vines, with unblinking commitment, so artfully honors it: whereas "Above All That?" alludes, deceptively— via "Mary of Magdala"'s remarks upon her ostensible opposite number, "the dolorous Mother of God"— to the Immaculate Conception (as it is popularly misconceived), "Blinky" alludes—via Oakland Raiders "Frederick Biletnikoff" (#25) and "Snake" (Ken Stabler, #12, whose nickname, in turn, recalls the event which necessitated the Immaculate Conception, etc.; Renaissance artists often depicted the Tree of Life in the Garden of Eden as an oak; Stabler often fraternized with members of the Hells Angels)— to the "Immaculate Reception" perpetrated by their ostensible opposite numbers on the Pittsburgh Steelers, Franco Harris (#32) and Terry Bradshaw (#12, "The Blonde Bomber")—with the unintended assistance of Raider Jack "The Assassin" Tatum (#32), and Steeler John "Frenchy" Fuqua (#33), the intended receiver—in an AFC Divisional Playoff Game on the eve of Christmas Eve, 1972 (mere weeks earlier, Merrill's *Braving the Elements* had been awarded the Bollingen Prize by a panel of judges including Anthony Hecht). Besides, if not above, all that, the utterances of "Blinky"'s opening line—"Grouseleachy," "housebeachy"— eerily evoke, even to the leeriest ear, and especially as compounded with the "Mullet on fire" of the penultimate line, both the word "louse" and the beach houses of Fire Island, and consequently— enhancing the effect of Franco Harris' signaled (if, perhaps, less than fair) catch— Frank O'Hara's fairly singular *cachet*. As O'Hara informed John (Lawrence) Ashbery, the title of his poem "Louise" (written in 1959, the year of the Oakland Raiders' inception, as the "Oakland Señors;" Bradshaw attended Louisiana Tech) derives from "a louse I saw in the john... on my immaculate person;" and O'Hara died on Fire Island in the summer of 1966, mere weeks after the Double Dactyl was debuted in *Esquire* magazine ("Blinky"'s graceful scoring of the *pas de deux* between quarterback and receiver, by which balletic Biletnikoff—born of Russian parents—demonstrates his dual nature, also acknowledges another "Mr. B"— George Balanchine, of whose New York City Ballet O'Hara, along with his former college roommate, Edward Gorey, was a passionate devotee). Furthermore, "Blinky" receives within its ever-stabilizing ken two figures whose names are eligible to be (though are not, as yet) immortalized by the Double Dactyl, Raiders quarterback Daryle Lamonica

("The Mad Bomber;" alma mater: Notre Dame), who, the season after the "Immaculate Reception," ceded his starting position to Stabler; and William R. Wilkerson—the founder of the *Hollywood Reporter*, Sunset Strip restaurateur, and alleged blacklister who famously discovered Lana Turner, precipitating her ascent, etc. Cathy Wilkerson, of solely hypothetical relation to William, is the woman portrayed in these lines from "18 West 11th Street" (11-18= -7, the result of the "Immaculate Reception" on the Raiders' point differential), Merrill's poem (first collected in *Braving the Elements*) about his childhood home, which was blown apart by members of the Weathermen: "…She stirs, she moans the name / Adam. And is *gone*…"

9. cf. "High Art," by John Hollander. *Jiggery-Pokery: A Compendium of Double Dactyls* (Atheneum, 1967), p. 112.

CONTRIBUTORS

AUSTIN ALLEN's first collection, *Pleasures of the Game* (Waywiser Press, 2016), won the eleventh Anthony Hecht Poetry Prize. His poems and essays have appeared widely. He lives and teaches in Cincinnati.

GILBERT ALLEN'S most recent books are *Catma* and *The Final Days of Great American Shopping*. A longtime resident of upstate South Carolina, he is the Bennette E. Geer Professor of Literature Emeritus at Furman University.

JAMES ARTHUR's poems have appeared in *The New Yorker*, *The New York Review of Books*, *Poetry*, *Narrative*, and *The New Republic*. His first book, *Charms Against Lightning*, was published by Copper Canyon Press in 2012. Arthur has received the Amy Lowell Travelling Poetry Scholarship, a Stegner Fellowship, a Hodder Fellowship, and a Discovery/*The Nation* Award. He lives in Baltimore, where he teaches in the Writing Seminars at Johns Hopkins University.

KENNETH BLEETH is professor emeritus of English at Connecticut College.

KIM BRIDGFORD is the author of nine books of poetry, including *Human Interest*. She has been the recipient of grants from the NEA, the Connecticut Commission on the Arts, and the Ucross Foundation, and has been honored by The Baldwin School, along with Marilyn Nelson and Faith Ringgold, for her contributions to women's writing. In a literary career spanning thirty-five years, her values of inclusive community and women's history have forged two important new literary institutions: Poetry by the Sea: A Global Conference and Mezzo Cammin.In 2010, she launched The Mezzo Cammin Women Poets Timeline Project at the National Museum of Women in the Arts in Washington, and went on to hold events at the Pennsylvania Academy of the Fine Arts and at Fordham University-Lincoln Center. With visual artist Jo Yarrington, she is the author of a three-volume series, *The Falling Edge*, about their journeys to Iceland, Venezuela, and Bhutan. Their current project, The Rotating Axis, will take them to Antarctica, the Seychelles, and Greenland. With Russell Goings, she rang the closing bell of the New York Stock Exchange, in honor of his book *The Children of Children Keep Coming*, for which she wrote the introduction. She is known as "America's First Lady of Form."

GEOFFREY BROCK is the author of two volumes of verse, *Weighing Light* and *Voices Bright Flags*. He is also the editor of the *FSG Book of 20th-Century Italian Poetry* and the translator of several books of Italian poetry and prose. He lives and teaches in Schmarkansas, Arkansas.

BRIAN BRODEUR is the author of the poetry collections *Natural Causes* (2012) and *Other Latitudes* (2008), as well as the chapbooks *Local Fauna* (2015) and *So the Night Cannot Go on Without Us* (2007). He is Assistant Professor of English at Indiana University East, where he coordinates the Veterans Writing Workshop of Richmond, Indiana.

GUY BENJAMIN BROOKSHIRE is the author of *The Universe War*, a collage comic book, and *New Oldestland* (421 Atlanta Press, 2014). His podcast, *The Republic of Sin: A Post-Colonial Horror Fantasy*, is available at republicofsin.com and on iTunes.

TERESE COE's poems and translations have appeared in *The Threepenny Review, Poetry, New American Writing, Ploughshares, Alaska Quarterly Review, The Cincinnati Review, Poetry Review*, the *TLS, Agenda, Warwick Review, The Moth, The Stinging Fly*, and many other publications. Her most recent collection of poems and translations is Kelsay Books' *Shot Silk*, which was listed for the 2017 Poet's Prize. Links to additional information and work can be found at http://en.wikipedia.org/wiki/Terese_Coe

ALFRED CORN is the author of eleven books of poems, the most recent titled *Unions*. In 2014, he published his second novel, titled *Miranda's Book*. He is the recipient of awards from the Guggenheim Foundation, the Academy of American Poets, the American Academy of Arts and Letters, and the NEA.

KEVIN CRAFT is the author of the poetry collections *Solar Prominence* (Cloudbank Books, 2005) and *Vagrants & Accidentals* (University of Washington Press, 2017). He is the director of the Written Arts Program at Everett Community College, and teaches in the University of Washington's Creative Writing in Rome Program.

JAMES CUMMINS was born in Ohio and grew up in the Midwest. He attended the Iowa Writers› Workshop. His first book, *The Whole Truth*, a sequence of sestinas about the Perry Mason characters, was reissued in 2003 in the Classic Contemporary Series at Carnegie Mellon University Press. His other books include *Portrait in a Spoon, Then & Now, Jim and Dave Defeat the Masked Man* (co-authored with David Lehman), and *Still Some Cake*. He is curator of the Elliston Poetry Collection at the University of Cincinnati, and is married to the poet Maureen Bloomfield.

JOHN DRURY is the author of four books of poetry: *Sea Level Rising* (Able Muse Press, 2015), *The Refugee Camp* (Turning Point Books, 2011), *Burning the Aspern Papers* (Miami University Press, 2003), and *The Disappearing Town* (Miami University Press, 2000). His awards include a Pushcart Prize, two Ohio Arts Council grants, an Ingram Merrill Foundation fellowship, and the Bernard F. Conners Prize from the *Paris Review*. He is a Professor of English at the University of Cincinnati.

JOHN DUVAL teaches as the James E. and Ellen Wadley Roper Professor of Creative Writing/ Translation at the University of Arkansas. He has received both the Harold Morton Landon Translation Award and the Raissiz/de Palchi Award in Italian Translation from the Academy of American Poets. His Song of Roland was short-listed for the PEN/USA translation award in 2013.

ANNIE FINCH is the author of six books of poetry, including *Eve, Calendars*, and *Spells: New and Selected Poems*. Her poems have appeared in the *Penguin Book of Twentieth-Century American Poetry* and onstage at Carnegie Hall. Her verse play on abortion, *Among the Goddesses: An Epic Libretto in Seven Dreams,* received the Sarasvati Award for Poetry, and she has been honored with the Robert Fitzgerald Award for her lifetime contribution to the field of prosody and poetic form. She teaches in the low-residency MFA program at St. Francis College in Brooklyn.

JOHN FULLER is a poet, novelist and critic ('A significant presence in

British letters': *The Times*). He is an Emeritus Fellow of Magdalen College, Oxford, where for many years he was Tutor in English. Chatto and Windus published his *Collected Poems* and his most recent books, *Gravel in my Shoe* and *The Bone Flowers*. His collected double-dactyls will appear from Shoestring Press this year.

MICHAEL GRIFFITH's books are *Trophy, Bibliophilia: A Novella and Stories,* and *Spikes: A Novel.* He is Professor of English at the University of Cincinnati and Fiction Editor of the *Cincinnati Review*. He is also the Editor of *Yellow Shoe Fiction*, an original-fiction series from LSU Press.

DANIEL GROVES slept as (REDACTED), the Russian Blue, purr-sang in hot pursuit ("*Da. Pur et chic*"): "Turncoat duplicities! Intra-reconnaissance putting a tail on me (*Da.* I will shake)."

HASTINGS HENSEL is the author of *Winter Inlet*, winner of the 2014-2015 Unicorn Press First Book Prize, and the chapbook *Control Burn*, winner of the *Iron Horse Literary Review* 2011 Single-Author Contest. His poems have appeared in *storySouth, The Greensboro Review, Cave Wall, 32 Poems*, and elsewhere. He lives in Murrells Inlet, SC and teaches in the English Department at Coastal Carolina University.

JAIMEE HILLS is the author of *How to Avoid Speaking*, winner of the tenth Anthony Hecht Poetry Prize. Her poems have appeared in *Best New Poets, Mississippi Review, Drunken Boat, Blackbird*, and elsewhere. She teaches at Marquette University and lives in Milwaukee, WI.

ANDREW HUDGINS is the author of, most recently, *The Joker: A Memoir* (Simon and Schuster, 2013), *A Clown at Midnight* (Harcourt Houghton Mifflin, 2013), and *American Rendering: New and Selected Poems* (Harcourt Houghton Mifflin, 2010). He is retired from Ohio State University and lives in Sewanee, Tennessee.

A. M. JUSTER's most recent books are: *Tibullus' Elegies* (Oxford University Press, 2012), *Saint Aldhelm's Riddles* (University of Toronto Press, 2015), *Sleaze & Slander: New and Selected Comic Verse 1995-2015* (Measure Press, 2016), and *The Billy Collins Experience* (Kelsay Books, 2016).

J. KATES is a poet, literary translator and the president and co-director of Zephyr Press, a non-profit press that focuses on contemporary works in translation from Russia, Eastern Europe and Asia. He has been awarded a National Endowment for the Arts Creative Writing Fellowship in Poetry, a Translation Project Fellowship, an Individual Artist Fellowship from the New Hampshire State Council on the Arts and the Cliff Becker Book Prize in Translation for the *Selected Poems* of Mikhail Yeryomin (White Pine Press, 2014). He has published three chapbooks of his own poems: *Mappemonde* (Oyster River Press, 2014) *Metes and Bounds* (Accents Publishing, 2010) and *The Old Testament* (Cold Hub Press, 2015) and a full book, *The Briar Patch* (Hobblebush Books, 2012).

SEAN KELLY is an Anglophone Quebecois in exile in Brooklyn, NY. In his youth he was partially responsible for numerous books and TV scripts. Against all odds, he has nine grand daughters.

X. J. KENNEDY's most recent books are *In a Prominent Bar in Secaucus: New & Selected Poems* (ALA Notable Book); *Fits of Concision: Collected Poems of Six or Fewer Lines*; a comic novel *A Hoarse Half-human Cheer*; and (with Dana Gioia) *An Introduction to Poetry, 13th Edition*. In 2015 Poets & Writers gave him the Jackson Poetry Prize.

RICHARD KENNEY's most recent book is *The One-Strand River* (Knopf, 2008). He teaches at the University of Washington.

BRAD LEITHAUSER's most recent book is *The Oldest Word for Dawn: New and Selected Poems* (Knopf, 2013).

WILLIAM LOGAN's new book of poetry is *Rift of Light* (Penguin, 2017).

J. D. McCLATCHY is the author of eight collections of poetry, most recently *Plundered Hearts: New and Selected Poems* (Knopf, 2014, and Waywiser, 2016). He is the author or editor of dozens of other books, and has written sixteen libretti performed at leading opera houses around the world, including the Metropolitan Opera, Covent Garden, and La Scala. Until his retirement this year, he taught at Yale and served as editor of the *Yale Review*.

JENNIFER MAIER's most recent book of poems is *Now, Now* (University of Pittsburgh Press, 2013). Her first collection, *Dark Alphabet*, won the Crab Orchard Review Series in Poetry First Book Award and was named one of the Ten Remarkable Books of 2006 by the Academy of American

Poets. Her poetry has appeared in numerous literary journals, including *Poetry, American Poet, Poetry Daily,* and *Christianity & Literature,* and has been featured several times on Public Radio International's *The Writer's Almanac* hosted by Garrison Keillor.

CHARLES MARTIN's seventh book of poems, *Future Perfect*, will be published in the spring of 2018 by The Johns Hopkins University Press. His verse translation of the *Metamorphoses of Ovid* (W. W. Norton & Co., 2004) received the Harold Morton Landon Award from the Academy of American Poets. In 2005, he received an Award for Literature from the American Academy of Arts and Letters. He served as Poet in Residence at The Cathedral of St. John the Divine in New York from 2005 to 2009.

ERIC McHENRY grew up in Topeka, Kansas and earned degrees from Beloit College and Boston University. His first book of poems, *Potscrubber Lullabies* (Waywiser, 2006), won the Kate Tufts Discovery Award, and in 2010 *Poetry Northwest* awarded him the Theodore Roethke Prize. He is a contributing editor of *Columbia* magazine and has written about poetry for the *New York Times Book Review, Parnassus: Poetry in Review*, the *San Francisco Chronicle*, the *Boston Globe and Slate*. He lives in Topeka with his wife, Sonja, and their two children, Evan and Sage, and teaches creative writing at Washburn University. In 2015 he was appointed Poet Laureate of Kansas.

ALFRED NICOL has published three books of poetry: *Winter Light,* which received the 2004 Richard Wilbur Award; *Elegy for Everyone*, published in 2009; and *Animal Psalms,* published by Able Muse Press in 2016.

JACQUELINE OSHEROW's most recent collection of poems is *Ultimatum from Paradise* (LSU Press, 2014).

ROBERT SCHREUR works at Johns Hopkins Bayview Medical Center and as a psychotherapist in private practice. A volume of his selected poems, *That Said,* will be published in 2017.

NATALIE SHAPERO is the Professor of the Practice of Poetry at Tufts University and the author of *Hard Child* (Saturnalia Books, 2013) and *No Object* (Copper Canyon Press, 2017).

WILLARD SPIEGELMAN is the Hughes Professor emeritus at Southern

Methodist University in Dallas. From 1984 until 2016, he was also the editor in chief of *Southwest Review*. He has written many books and essays about English and American poetry. For more than a quarter century he has been a regular contributor to the Leisure & Arts pages of *The Wall Street Journal*. His two latest books are *Senior Moments: Looking Back, Looking Ahead* (Farrar Straus and Giroux, 2016) and *If You See Something, Say Something: A Writer Looks at Art* (DeGolyer Library, SMU, 2016).

PHILIP STEPHENS is the author of *Miss Me When I'm Gone: A Novel* (Plume Editions, 2011) and the poetry collection *The Determined Days* (Overlook Press, 2000), which was a finalist for the PEN Center USA West Literary Award. His work has appeared in *The Oxford American, Southwest Review*, and *Bomb*, among other publications, as well as in Da Capo Best Music Writing 2004. He lives with his wife and sons in Kansas City, MO.

JUDITH TESTA was born in New York and came to Chicago to attend graduate school at the University of Chicago, where she received MA and PhD degrees. She is a retired professor who taught history of art at Northern Illinois University in DeKalb from 1969 until 2000. She is the author of two scholarly books and numerous academic articles. Since retiring, she has been spending at least two months of each year in Rome, the place she calls "the city of my soul." She now writes book reviews, travel and history pieces for *Fra Noi*, the monthly magazine of the greater Chicago area Italian American community. She has also written three books for more general audiences: *Rome Is Love Spelled Backward, Sal Maglie: Baseball's Demon Barber*, and *An Art Lover's Guide to Florence*.

ADAM VINES is an Assistant Professor at the University of Alabama at Birmingham, where he is Editor of *Birmingham Poetry Review*, Director of the English Honors Program, and Faculty Advisor of the UAB Fishing Team. He has published recent poems in *The Kenyon Review, Poetry, Southwest Review, Gulf Coast*, and *Measure*. He is author of *The Coal Life* (University of Arkansas Press, 2012) and coauthor of *According to Discretion* (Unicorn Press, 2015).

CODY WALKER is the author of *The Trumpiad* (Waywiser, 2017), *The Self-Styled No-Child* (Waywiser, 2016), *Shuffle and Breakdown* (Waywiser, 2008), and the co-editor of *Alive at the Center: Contemporary Poems from the Pacific Northwest* (Ooligan, 2013). He lives with his family in Ann

Arbor, where he teaches English at the University of Michigan.

CHRIS WALLACE-CRABBE is an Australian poet. A sometime Harkness Poetry Fellow in poetry at Yale, he has taught at Harvard and the University of Melbourne. His latest volume of poetry is *Afternoon in the Central Nervous System* (George Braziller, New York, 2015).

CAKI WILKINSON is the author of the poetry collections *Circles Where the Head Should Be* (UNT, 2011) and *The Wynona Stone Poems* (Persea, 2015). She lives in Memphis, TN.

GREG (WESLEY) WILLIAMSON, *oppidum fatuus*, puts on his cape in a telephone booth, launching his one-person counterinsurgency: "They will not, Goddammit, silence the truth."

DAVID YEZZI's most recent books of poems are *Birds of the* Air, and, forthcoming in 2018, *Black Sea*, both from Carnegie Mellon. He is chair of the Writing Seminars at Johns Hopkins and editor of *The Hopkins Review*.

Other Books from Waywiser

POETRY
Austin Allen, *Pleasures of the Game*
Al Alvarez, *New & Selected Poems*
Chris Andrews, *Lime Green Chair*
George Bradley, *A Few of Her Secrets*
Geoffrey Brock, *Voices Bright Flags*
Robert Conquest, *Blokelore & Blokesongs*
Robert Conquest, *Penultimata*
Morri Creech, *Field Knowledge*
Morri Creech, *The Sleep of Reason*
Peter Dale, *One Another*
Erica Dawson, *Big-Eyed Afraid*
B. H. Fairchild, *The Art of the Lathe*
David Ferry, *On This Side of the River: Selected Poems*
Jeffrey Harrison, *The Names of Things: New & Selected Poems*
Joseph Harrison, *Identity Theft*
Joseph Harrison, *Shakespeare's Horse*
Joseph Harrison, *Someone Else's Name*
Joseph Harrison, ed., *The Hecht Prize Anthology, 2005-2009*
Anthony Hecht, *Collected Later Poems*
Anthony Hecht, *The Darkness and the Light*
Jaimee Hills, *How to Avoid Speaking*
Hilary S. Jacqmin, *Missing Persons*
Carrie Jerrell, *After the Revival*
Stephen Kampa, *Articulate as Rain*
Stephen Kampa, *Bachelor Pad*
Rose Kelleher, *Bundle o' Tinder*
Mark Kraushaar, *The Uncertainty Principle*
Matthew Ladd, *The Book of Emblems*
J. D. McClatchy, *Plundered Hearts: New and Selected Poems*
Dora Malech, *Shore Ordered Ocean*
Jérôme Luc Martin, *The Gardening Fires: Sonnets and Fragments*
Eric McHenry, *Odd Evening*
Eric McHenry, *Potscrubber Lullabies*
Eric McHenry and Nicholas Garland, *Mommy Daddy Evan Sage*
Timothy Murphy, *Very Far North*
Ian Parks, *Shell Island*
V. Penelope Pelizzon, *Whose Flesh is Flame, Whose Bone is Time*
Chris Preddle, *Cattle Console Him*
Shelley Puhak, *Guinevere in Baltimore*
Christopher Ricks, ed., *Joining Music with Reason:
34 Poets, British and American, Oxford 2004-2009*
Daniel Rifenburgh, *Advent*
Mary Jo Salter, *It's Hard to Say: Selected Poems*

Other Books from Waywiser

W. D. Snodgrass, *Not for Specialists: New & Selected Poems*
Mark Strand, *Almost Invisible*
Mark Strand, *Blizzard of One*
Bradford Gray Telford, *Perfect Hurt*
Matthew Thorburn, *This Time Tomorrow*
Cody Walker, *Shuffle and Breakdown*
Cody Walker, *The Self-Styled No-Child*
Cody Walker, *The Trumpiad*
Deborah Warren, *The Size of Happiness*
Clive Watkins, *Already the Flames*
Clive Watkins, *Jigsaw*
Mike White, *Addendum to a Miracle*
Richard Wilbur, *Anterooms*
Richard Wilbur, *Mayflies*
Richard Wilbur, *Collected Poems 1943-2004*
Norman Williams, *One Unblinking Eye*
Greg Williamson, *A Most Marvelous Piece of Luck*
Greg Williamson, *The Hole Story of Kirby the Sneak and Arlo the True*
Stephen Yenser, *Stone Fruit*

FICTION

Gregory Heath, *The Entire Animal*
Mary Elizabeth Pope, *Divining Venus*
K. M. Ross, *The Blinding Walk*
Gabriel Roth, *The Unknowns**
Matthew Yorke, *Chancing It*

ILLUSTRATED

Nicholas Garland, *I wish ...*
Eric McHenry and Nicholas Garland, *Mommy Daddy Evan Sage*
Greg Williamson, *The Hole Story of Kirby the Sneak and Arlo the True*

NON-FICTION

Neil Berry, *Articles of Faith: The Story of British Intellectual Journalism*
Mark Ford, *A Driftwood Altar: Essays and Reviews*
Ed. Philip Hoy, *A Bountiful Harvest:*
The Correspondence of Anthony Hecht and William L. MacDonald
Richard Wollheim, *Germs: A Memoir of Childhood*

* Co-published with Picador